David's World

By Jan M. Mike

Contents

Celebrat
Pearson Lea. W9-AUK-037

Meet David

When David was born, no one could see that he was different from most children. You probably couldn't see it now. However, he was missing some tiny hairs in his **inner ear**, which are very important. Their job is to move sound through the inner ear into the brain.

The **cochlea** is a snail-shaped, liquid-filled tube in the inner ear. Inside the cochlea tiny hairs carry sound signals to the **auditory nerve**, which sends messages to the brain. The brain sorts out the messages, and we hear sounds.

David was born without enough of those tiny hairs in his inner ears. For that reason David is deaf.

David Metcalf as a young child

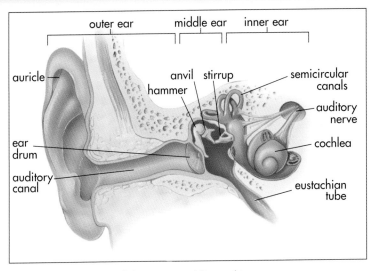

Parts of the outer, middle, and inner ear

Sound waves travel into the ears every moment of every day. These vibrations travel along the **auditory canal**. The **eardrum** vibrates when the sound waves reach it.

From there three tiny bones in the **middle ear** take over the job of sending sound vibrations to the brain. The hammer, anvil, and stirrup are very small bones that form a bridge between the eardrum and the small opening to the inner ear. As a team, these bones are called **ossicles**. They pass the vibrations into the cochlea, where tiny hairs change them into signals called impulses. These impulses are sent by the auditory nerve to the brain.

A Surprising Discovery

In 1959, when David was born, babies were not tested for hearing loss, as they are now. As time passed, David's parents knew something was different about him, but they didn't know what it was. He didn't seem to pay attention as well as his older brother and sister. He seldom tried to speak, and when he did, his words were hard to understand. His parents didn't know then that David was deaf and that he had taught himself to read lips. That is how he managed to communicate.

David started school when he was six years old. His kindergarten teacher was the first to realize David was hearing impaired. A hearing test confirmed her suspicions. David had **sensorineural hearing loss**, often called nerve deafness. His parents were confused and afraid and took David to doctors all over their state, looking for a cure. They had trouble accepting that their child was deaf.

David could feel their emotional upset and sadness, but for him nothing important had changed. His world still included friends and baseball, school and swimming. It did not include sound, but it never had. He had learned to communicate without it. Then his father made a decision that nearly changed David's world forever.

These children are "talking" to one another using sign language.

One day David's father drove him from their small town to the American School for the Deaf in the nearby city of West Hartford, Connecticut. They walked into a classroom. After a few minutes the teacher told David's father he should go, so he left David there and went to work.

Although children filled the room, David felt alone. Everyone stared at him; everything looked strange. The ceiling was too high. The lights were too bright. The walls were the wrong color, and the books were in the wrong places. Worst of all, the other children were making strange signs in the air with their hands.

David did not like this new class at all. Not one of his friends was there to help him understand what the teacher wanted him to do. Without his friends he felt lost and lonely.

David told the teacher he wanted to leave. She tried her best to comfort him, telling him he would be fine. But as the day went on, David wasn't fine.

He felt angry and afraid. People here talked with their hands instead of their mouths. They didn't understand him when he tried to speak to them. David knew he had to make the teacher send him back home, and quickly.

He climbed on top of a table and began to throw things. Books, lunchboxes, paper and pencils—he threw everything he could reach. He refused to stop until the teacher called his father.

"What is going on?" David's father asked when he arrived to pick David up.

David answered, "I don't like that place," but he couldn't make his dad understand why.

When he got home, David told his mother he was never going back to that school again.

"Okay," his mother said. "We'll see what we can do."

David returned to his old school the very next day.

A Hearing Aid

A few weeks later David's parents got him a hearing aid—a box-type one with a large microphone to catch sounds. It had earplugs that passed sounds into his ears. For the first time David could hear!

But the hearing aid was bulky and heavy, and it made all sounds louder—even the unimportant ones. The ticking of the clock was just as loud as his teacher's voice, sometimes louder.

Since David had never heard sounds before, his brain couldn't tell the difference between the many noises the hearing aid was picking up. The noises were a loud jumble, and the jumble made no sense to him at all. Soon David tucked the hearing aid away in a drawer and forgot about it.

This young boy wears a box-type hearing aid.

David's mother worked with him for hours every day, helping him to improve his lip-reading techniques. At first she taught him the names of objects. She would write a word like *cup* on a piece of paper and then show David a cup. Together they would repeat the word.

Although David was smart and really wanted to succeed, school was difficult. Every time the teacher turned around to write on the board, David was lost because he could no longer read her lips.

His parents hired a tutor for him, and his mother drilled him on his math. She also introduced him to new words every day. David borrowed friends' notes and worked very hard. Yet he also made time for football, baseball, wrestling, and reading.

Unlike some hearing-impaired children, David loved to read. Because they can't hear, deaf children may have difficulty acquiring language skills. But because of the work he had done with his mother, David had an unusually advanced vocabulary. He continued to increase it by reading all kinds of books, especially mysteries, westerns, and science fiction. Books answered many of his questions and helped him escape for a while.

A group of hearing-impaired children having fun at school

Being Deaf Today

David's early life might have been quite different had he been born today. Now doctors check infants' hearing so treatment can begin early for any hearing loss. Specially trained people visit the children's homes to teach parents about deafness, and school programs help deaf children learn language.

Now there are far more options for deaf children. Some may be helped by surgery, and others, by new state-of-the-art hearing aids. One surgical option is a **cochlear implant**, a tiny electronic device implanted in the ear. Even external hearing aids are much smaller and lighter now than David's was.

Children who can benefit from hearing aids now usually begin using them at a young age. They grow up hearing sounds, and their brains learn how to interpret those sounds.

Another option is special schools for deaf children, where there are teachers trained to meet their special needs. This special school community helps each child grow and learn and form strong friendships. In such an environment, hearing loss doesn't make students feel different. Deaf students put out the yearbook, act in the plays, run the student government, and are star athletes.

Other deaf children choose to "mainstream," to go to schools that have large numbers of hearing children and share classes with them. This is what David chose to do. Some mainstreamed deaf children have sign-language interpreters to help them in school. Others have tutors or note takers to help.

Deciding where to attend school is a big decision for hearing-impaired children and their families. There are many things to consider. How much hearing does a student have? How far away is the school? Where will the student be happiest and learn the most? Students, parents, doctors, teachers, and counselors are all involved in making the decision.

Into the Deaf Community

After David graduated from high school, he left home for college and found a new world. At college he learned how to sign, or communicate using American Sign Language. It uses the hands and body to show words and letters. Common words and phrases have their own special hand signs or body movements called gestures. Less common words are spelled out letter by letter, using the sign alphabet in which each letter has a special hand shape. Gestures are easy to understand, such as shivering for "cold."

After he learned to sign, David used a sign-language interpreter, who signed to him what his teachers were saying. That helped him get better grades.

Here are the hand positions for each letter of the alphabet.

Learning sign language did far more than help David get better grades. It also opened a door for him. For the first time he became part of a community of other people like him, who were deaf.

In this community, deafness is not only about hearing loss. It is a state of being and an identity. These deaf people do not see hearing loss as a handicap. They see themselves as members of a group that has a special way of life. Even the way the word is written can be important: *Deaf* with a capital *D* refers to life in the Deaf community, while *deaf* with a small *d* refers to the hearing loss itself.

In college David had deaf friends for the first time. He enjoyed sign-language jokes. He went to Deaf stage plays and enjoyed Deaf music.

Deaf music is enjoyed mostly by sight. Dancers express feelings and stories—some special to the Deaf community, others familiar to hearing people also. The music helps the dancers follow the same rhythm. Some dancers can hear the beat; others feel it through vibrations in the floor. A few need hand signs to help them time their movements.

David is an adult now and an active member of both the hearing and Deaf communities. He works as an architect and dreams of living in a place where deaf and hearing people can communicate easily.

Such communities have existed in the past. On the island of Martha's Vineyard, Massachusetts, there was once a large deaf population after deaf settlers arrived in the 1690s. In some villages one person in four was deaf. Both hearing and deaf people knew how to communicate using sign language. No one felt left out or different because of a hearing loss. Because the deaf people had an excellent free education at the state school for the deaf, they were sometimes better educated than the hearing people. Their hearing neighbors often went to them for advice.

Even today, with fewer deaf residents, some older hearing people in Martha's Vineyard still sign to each other. Some say they even dream in sign language.

In communities like Tisbury in Martha's Vineyard, both hearing and deaf people once communicated using sign language.

Dad, Can You Hear Me?

A few years after he finished college, David got married. His wife, Judy, is a hearing person who learned sign language. They have a daughter named Kimbrel, or Kim for short.

Kim realized her father was deaf when she was four years old. She knew earlier that he had trouble hearing, but then she began to suspect he was reading her lips. One day she covered her mouth and talked to him. He asked what she had said. She tried the experiment again, and her father couldn't understand her. Kim then knew that her father could not hear her voice.

David, with his daughter, Kim

At first Kim was both frightened and sad. This is a very normal reaction for hearing children who have deaf parents. Some children worry that their parents' deafness might be contagious, or catching. Could they become deaf from being near the parents? Could deafness make their parents sick, or even kill them? Kim wondered what would happen if she really needed her father to be able to hear her. She wondered if he could take care of her even if he couldn't hear her speak.

After a short time these worries melted away. Kim realized that nothing had really changed. Her father had always been deaf. He was not in any danger, and neither was she. David could read her lips, so communication was not a problem.

Kim can finger spell and knows some sign language. She can read signs for the letters of the alphabet quite well. She and her dad often watched television together, as hearing children might with hearing parents. There was one big difference though. David turned the sound off. In order to understand the program, Kim had to read the actors' lips. Now she can read lips as well as her father. When they want to communicate silently, they move their mouths without making a sound, and each knows what the other is saying.

Sometimes other children ask Kim a lot of questions about David. Why does your dad talk like that? Did he just lose his hearing? How do you talk to him? Their curiosity can sometimes be annoying for her. Like many children of deaf parents, Kim gets tired of answering the same questions over and over.

Even adults sometimes expect her to answer questions for her father, instead of asking David directly. She tries to be polite, telling the adults that her father is perfectly able to answer their questions.

While Kim can hear well, there was a good chance that she would have been born deaf like her father. Some deafness is hereditary. That means that a child of hearing-impaired parents is more likely to be born deaf than a child of hearing parents is. Early testing relieved Kim's parents' concerns.

Still, like many children of deaf parents, Kim wondered what it would be like to be deaf herself. She had a chance to find out more about not being able to hear when a visitor came to her school to teach about deafness. He brought specially designed earmuffs that blocked out all sound. The children put on the earmuffs, and then they tried to guess what other people were saying. Kim didn't need to guess. Since she could lip-read, she knew what people said. Her friends and her teacher were very impressed!

Help From Technology

About 3 persons out of 1,000 in the United States are born with mild to total hearing loss. There are two major kinds. **Conductive hearing loss** results from anything that blocks sound from reaching the inner ear, from illness to accident. It can be treated with surgery, medicine, and hearing aids. Sensorineural hearing loss results from damage to the hair cells or nerves of the inner ear. Hearing aids may help.

An **audiologist** specializes in testing people's hearing. After determining the extent of hearing loss, an audiologist can suggest the best type of hearing aid for a patient. Unlike David's large one, hearing aids now are quite small and very effective.

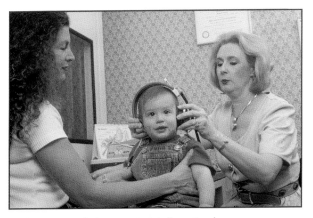

An audiologist is specially trained to test a person's ability to hear.

In the mid-1990s, David began to read about a surgical operation called a cochlear implant, which has helped many people. He called an audiologist to learn more. He took several hearing tests and afterward tried a new hearing aid, which helped him hear. His doctor believed that a cochlear implant might help him hear even better.

Hearing aids make sounds louder or clearer. Since they don't help sound get to the brain, they can't help some types of hearing loss. But a cochlear implant sends electrical signals along the auditory nerve to the brain. For those with sensorineural hearing loss, like David, it can mean a chance to hear sounds that are more like those that hearing people experience.

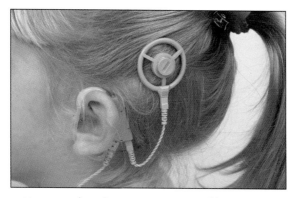

Many people with severe sensorineural hearing loss have been helped by a cochlear implant.

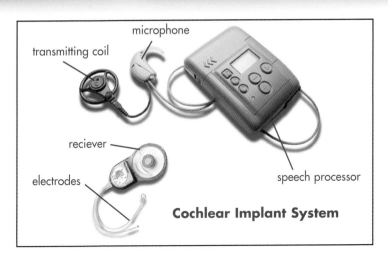

microphone

transmitting coil

reciever

electrodes

speech processor

Cochlear Implant System

When a person gets a cochlear implant, a surgeon inserts a small receiver under the skin near the ear. It is attached to very thin wires, called **electrodes**, which are placed in the cochlea.

Sound is picked up by a small microphone worn behind the ear and travels along a thin cord to a speech processor. This processor is a tiny computer usually carried in a person's pocket. It changes the sound into electrical signals.

These signals are sent to a transmitting coil, also worn behind the ear, and then into the implanted receiver. The receiver sends the signals to electrodes in the cochlea. The electrodes stimulate the auditory nerve, which sends the sound messages to the brain to be interpreted.

After his cochlear implant David could really hear, but he had to teach his brain what these new signals meant. Hearing people can make sense of what they hear because their brains are used to sound. David, however, had heard no sounds as a child. His brain could interpret tiny facial movements, so he could read lips. It could also interpret the hand movements of sign language. But his brain had to learn how to hear.

Judy and Kim help him practice hearing. They cover their mouths and read to him. This way he can't lip-read. Then they ask him to repeat what they've said. Sometimes he isn't sure and guesses. When his guesses are funny, everyone laughs— including David. Slowly and surely his brain is learning what each sound means.

A newly hearing person must learn to make sense of the many sounds in our world.

Although David thinks his cochlear implant is fantastic, hearing can be stressful for him. There are times when he misses the peace of his silent world.

Cochlear implants are not for all deaf people. While many deaf children have had implants, many parents prefer to wait until their children are old enough to decide for themselves whether to have an implant. Surgery always has some health risks, and some parents feel the risks outweigh the benefits.

Others see no reason to turn a deaf child into a hearing child. They accept their child's deafness as a special part of who that child is and often see little benefit in making their children hear. They feel that deafness is not a disease to be cured. They see their children as members of a special group, living lives that are as rich and fulfilling as those of a hearing person. Why fix what isn't broken?

Hearing or not hearing, we all face life's challenges, and David knows that. "Whatever your goal is," David says, "you can achieve it. Don't let being deaf or being different get in your way. You don't know where life is going to take you. So have fun with your friends. If they're deaf, that just adds spice to your life. And if you want to do something, go out and do it."

Questions, Anyone?

Here are some of the most frequently asked questions and answers about deafness.

Question: Is American Sign Language the same across the United States?
Answer: There are small regional differences much like those in speaking. In some areas people say "soda," while in others they say "pop." Sign language differences are similar to these.

Question: How should I talk to a deaf person?
Answer: If a deaf person is with a hearing person, talk to both people. Most deaf people know how to communicate with hearing people. If the deaf person has an interpreter, talk to the deaf person, even if he or she watches the interpreter at times.

Having a conversation using sign language

When the deaf person answers, he or she will turn to you and speak. Be patient, and listen carefully. You might make a new friend.

Question: Aside from sign language and lip reading, how do deaf people communicate?
Answer: New technology has helped the Deaf community stay in touch. Computers, the Internet, e-mail, and other devices are important tools. Now deaf people do not need to rely on their hearing neighbors.

Question: Can deaf people use a telephone?
Answer: Some people with hearing loss have enough hearing to use a telephone. Others use a special device called a TTY, or Text Telephone, connected to a telephone, and they type in a message. There are special relay services that allow a deaf person using a TTY and telephone to contact someone using just a telephone. A trained operator reads the telephone message typed in by the deaf person. When the hearing person answers, the operator types the reply so the deaf person can read it.

Question: What causes deafness?
Answer: Some people, like David, are born deaf. Others may become deaf because of diseases, tumors, accidents, or loud noises—even loud music! As people age, they sometimes lose some hearing ability.

Glossary

audiologist an expert in testing people's hearing

auditory canal opening in the outer ear through which sound travels

auditory nerve the nerve that passes electrical impulses from the cochlea to the brain

cochlea snail-shaped, liquid-filled tube in the inner ear in which sound vibrations are changed into electrical impulses

cochlear implant tiny electronic device implanted into the ear to help deaf persons hear

conductive hearing loss hearing loss that is due mainly to disease or injury and is often temporary

eardrum thin membrane that separates the middle ear from the outer ear and vibrates when hit by sound waves

electrodes thin wires implanted in the cochlea that pass electrical signals to the auditory nerve

inner ear fluid-filled structure containing the organs for hearing and balance

middle ear air-filled structure containing the ossicles, which pass sound vibrations from the eardrum to the inner ear

ossicles the three tiny bones in the middle ear, which pass vibrations into the cochlea

sensorineural hearing loss permanent hearing loss usually caused by damage to hair cells in the inner ear or to the auditory nerve